BoardSource is dedicated to advancing the public good by building exceptional nonprofit boards and inspiring board service.

BoardSource was established in 1988 by the Association of Governing Boards of Universities and Colleges (AGB) and Independent Sector (IS). Prior to this, in the early 1980s, the two organizations had conducted a survey and found that although 30 percent of respondents believed they were doing a good job of board education and training, the rest of the respondents reported little, if any, activity in strengthening governance. As a result, AGB and IS proposed the creation of a new organization whose mission would be to increase the effectiveness of nonprofit boards.

With a lead grant from the Kellogg Foundation and funding from five other donors, BoardSource opened its doors in 1988 as the National Center for Nonprofit Boards with a staff of three and an operating budget of $385,000. On January 1, 2002, BoardSource took on its new name and identity. These changes were the culmination of an extensive process of understanding how we were perceived, what our audiences wanted, and how we could best meet the needs of nonprofit organizations.

Today, BoardSource is the premier voice of nonprofit governance. Its highly acclaimed products, programs, and services mobilize boards so that organizations fulfill their missions, achieve their goals, increase their impact, and extend their influence. BoardSource is a 501(c)(3) organization.

BoardSource provides

- resources to nonprofit leaders through workshops, training, and an extensive Web site (www.boardsource.org)
- governance consultants who work directly with nonprofit leaders to design specialized solutions to meet an organization's needs
- the world's largest, most comprehensive selection of material on nonprofit governance, including a large selection of books and CD-ROMs
- an annual conference that brings together approximately 900 governance experts, board members, and chief executives and senior staff from around the world

For more information, please visit our Web site at www.boardsource.org, e-mail us at mail@boardsource.org, or call us at 800-883-6262.

Have You Used These BoardSource Resources?

THE GOVERNANCE SERIES

1. *Ten Basic Responsibilities of Nonprofit Boards, Second Edition*
2. *Legal Responsibilities of Nonprofit Boards, Second Edition*
3. *Financial Responsibilities of Nonprofit Boards, Second Edition*
4. *Fundraising Responsibilities of Nonprofit Boards, Second Edition*
5. *The Nonprofit Board's Role in Mission, Planning, and Evaluation, Second Edition*
6. *Structures and Practices of Nonprofit Boards, Second Edition*

BOOKS

Navigating the Organizational Lifecycle: A Capacity-Building Guide for Nonprofit Leaders

Getting the Best from Your Board: An Executive's Guide to a Successful Partnership

The Nonprofit Dashboard: A Tool for Tracking Progress

Moving Beyond Founder's Syndrome to Nonprofit Success

Chief Executive Transitions: How to Hire and Support a Nonprofit CEO

Assessment of the Chief Executive

Nonprofit Executive Compensation: Planning, Performance, and Pay, Second Edition

The Board Chair Handbook, Second Edition

Taming the Troublesome Board Member

Culture of Inquiry: Healthy Debate in the Boardroom

Governance as Leadership: Reframing the Work of Nonprofit Boards

Understanding Nonprofit Financial Statements, Third Edition

The Nonprofit Board Answer Book: A Practical Guide for Board Members and Chief Executives, Second Edition

The Board Building Cycle: Nine Steps to Finding, Recruiting, and Engaging Nonprofit Board Members, Second Edition

The Nonprofit Legal Landscape

The Nonprofit Board's Guide to Bylaws

Managing Conflicts of Interest: A Primer for Nonprofit Boards, Second Edition

The Nonprofit Policy Sampler, Second Edition

The Source: Twelve Principles of Governance That Power Exceptional Boards

Fearless Fundraising for Nonprofit Boards, Second Edition

Who's Minding the Money? An Investment Guide for Nonprofit Board Members, Second Edition

DVDs

Meeting the Challenge: An Orientation to Nonprofit Board Service

Speaking of Money: A Guide to Fundraising for Nonprofit Board Members

ONLINE ASSESSMENTS

Board Self-Assessment

Assessment of the Chief Executive

Executive Search — Needs Assessment

For an up-to-date list of publications and information about current prices, membership, and other services, please call BoardSource at 800-883-6262 or visit our Web site at www.boardsource.org. For consulting services, please e-mail us at consulting@boardsource.org or call 877-892-6293.

CONTENTS

INTRODUCTION 1

CHAPTER 1: STRATEGIC PLANNING: DEFINITIONS AND BENEFITS 5
What Strategic Planning Is 5
What Strategic Planning Is Not 6
Why Organizations Should Plan 6
Ways to Address Common Concerns and Complaints 9

CHAPTER 2: THE PHASES OF STRATEGIC PLANNING 11
Phase 1 – Planning to Plan 11
Phase 2 – Understanding the Context 16
Phase 3 – Agreeing on Purpose and Direction 19
Phase 4 – Moving from Vision to Action 21
Phase 5 – Monitoring Progress 24

CHAPTER 3: PARTICIPANTS' ROLES AND RELATIONSHIPS 31
Key Stakeholders and Their Roles 31
Achieving Balance in the Process 37
Common Obstacles in Planning 38

CHAPTER 4: COMPONENTS OF A STRATEGIC PLAN 41
Who Gets What Version of the Strategic Plan? 41

CONCLUSION 45

APPENDIX I: RECRUITING THE STRATEGIC PLANNING TASK FORCE 47

APPENDIX II: CHARTERING THE STRATEGIC PLANNING TASK FORCE 49

APPENDIX III: METHODS OF GATHERING INPUT 52

APPENDIX IV: SAMPLE TREND ANALYSIS 54

APPENDIX V: SAMPLE VISION PRIORITIES, GOALS, AND ACTIONS 57

APPENDIX VI: *WORKSHEET FOR INVOLVING PARTICIPANTS* 59

APPENDIX VII: *HOW TO CHOOSE A STRATEGIC PLANNING CONSULTANT* 61

APPENDIX VIII: *SAMPLE CLIENT–CONSULTANT AGREEMENT* 65

APPENDIX IX: *ABOUT THE CD-ROM* 67

SUGGESTED RESOURCES 69

ABOUT THE AUTHOR 71

INTRODUCTION

Strategic planning. The process can be hard to visualize, unless you have been through it. Even if you're familiar with strategic planning, the effort probably conjures up thoughts of hard work, conflicting agendas, and endless meetings.

Strategic planning is all of those things, but the results are worth the effort. Leading the organization through the process of determining what it wants to be and how it will turn that ideal into a reality is one of the most important things a chief executive can do. Strategic planning allows the key stakeholders to get on the same page with respect to the organization's priorities and long- and short-term work. An organization's vision cannot be achieved until that happens.

An analogy may apply here: A ladder is a tool for reaching a destination that is not within reach without it. Climbing a ladder requires placing one foot after another on the rungs. Likewise, an organization might be productive and efficient — methodically climbing the ladder — without taking time to agree on a strategy for the future. There is little point, however, to such productivity and efficiency if, upon reaching the top of the ladder, you find yourself in the wrong place.

Strategic planning requires that before you buy the ladder and set foot on it, you have thought about where you are going and have had thoughtful conversations with others. Organizations that spend time thinking and debating *on a continuous basis* about where to place the ladder are more likely to be effective in planning and achieving their goals.

As the pivotal person in the organization, the chief executive initiates and guides the planning process with the board, staff, and community. This book was written for the nonprofit chief executive to help revise an existing strategic plan or begin the strategic planning process for the first time. The book will help

> *Before engaging in the strategic planning process, I had never understood its value. Without question, it is the reason for our program's expansion, income diversification, sustainability, and increased community awareness.*
>
> Suzanne Greenberg, Chief Executive, Child Abuse & Neglect Council of Saginaw, Michigan

- successfully obtain board support and participation in planning
- engage the right stakeholders at the right times in the planning process
- identify and manage the various phases in the process of strategic planning

The material presented here will *not* tell you what goes into your plan — it is not a do-it-yourself guide to content (for further information on strategic planning material, see the Suggested Resources section at the end of the book). The book *will* provide

- a roadmap to the comprehensive planning process with particular emphasis on the steps to take in order to optimize contributions from your board and staff

- advice about who to invite to the process and why

- guidance on how to structure and manage conversations with key stakeholders in order to create a new strategic framework for the organization

- ideas for how to extend the process to include continuous evaluation of how well the organization is staying focused on *planning* and *executing* the plan

Of course, strategic planning takes time. Strategic planning is most successful when the leaders driving the process recognize this and allow time for gathering data, discussing context, sharing ideas, and agreeing on what needs to be done. When staff and volunteers can see their own reflection in the plan that they helped create, they are more likely to commit time and energy to implement it. Throughout the book, the challenges of both chief executives and boards are illustrated with the story of Coats and Ties, a fictional nonprofit going through the strategic planning process.

Just as strategic planning follows a logical sequence to the creation of a written plan, the chapters of the book will lead you to a vision of what your plan could be.

Chapter 1 — Strategic Planning: Definitions and Benefits. The book begins by clarifying what strategic planning is and what it is not. This chapter provides a solid rationale for strategic planning that will help you make the case to others.

Chapter 2 — The Phases of Strategic Planning. Many people are confused about what steps to take to complete a strategic plan. This chapter takes you through the process and breaks it down into five phases.

Chapter 3 — Participants' Roles and Relationships. People are the most important element in strategic planning, and they need to be clear about their roles and their contributions. This chapter helps the chief executive find the right balance of managing people and process to foster agreement about the strategic plan.

Chapter 4 — Components of a Strategic Plan. So what does your strategic plan look like when you are finished? This chapter provides an outline to help you visualize the outcome of the planning process. The chapter not only prompts decisions about what will go in the plan but also helps you determine who should be involved.

In addition, the appendices provide a wealth of information to help you create a planning task force and choose a consultant. The appendices (listed below) also contain some useful samples and worksheets.

Appendix I — Recruiting the Strategic Planning Task Force

Appendix II — Chartering the Strategic Planning Task Force

Appendix III — Methods of Gathering Input

Appendix IV — Sample Trend Analysis

Appendix V — Sample Vision Priorities, Goals, and Actions

Appendix VI — Worksheet for Involving Participants

Appendix VII — How to Choose a Strategic Planning Consultant

Appendix VIII — Sample Client–Consultant Agreement

Appendix IX — About the CD-ROM

In the back of the book, you will find a CD-ROM called *Presenting: Strategic Planning — Choosing the Right Method for Your Nonprofit Organization.* This tool will help you and your board understand different approaches to strategic planning and choose the one that is most appropriate for your organization.

After reading this book, you should have:

- clarity about what strategic planning is and is not
- an understanding of why it is important to have a strategic plan
- enthusiasm to begin planning successfully
- commitment to plan and make planning a way of life in your organization

Ladders enable us to reach new heights. Similarly, the process of strategic planning can help your organization achieve its lofty goals. This book will help you get started.

CHAPTER 1
STRATEGIC PLANNING: DEFINITIONS AND BENEFITS

WHAT STRATEGIC PLANNING IS

It is helpful to have a definition of strategic planning. It is

- the process of defining a strategy for an organization with the greatest possible knowledge of its environment and context
- a written list of the actions needed to carry out the plan
- a method for monitoring the results achieved through the plan

Strategic planning is a disciplined approach to deciding what an organization is, what it does, and why it does it, with a focus on the future.[1] Strategic planning produces a framework that enables the organization to focus its energy, coordinate the efforts of individuals so that they are working toward the same goals, and assess the organization's response to changing factors and adjust accordingly.

It helps to think of the completed strategic plan as a "document of agreements" about the future of the organization and the steps to get there. The written plan is the reminder of the energetic dialogue that united the organization and resulted in important agreements. The written plan begins with the strategic focus and ends with documentation of "what's next" in the organization's future. A completed plan can reflect both long-range and operational thinking and can be a roadmap to future success.

A strategic plan contains

Mission Statement:	Why we exist
Vision:	What we want the organization to be in the future
Vision priorities:	How we will achieve the vision by focusing on the critical few areas of focus
Goals and Actions:	How we will, step by step, achieve each vision priority and, hence, the vision
Values:	How we will treat each other and our constituents

[1] Adapted from John M. Bryson, *Strategic Planning for Public and Nonprofit Organizations: A Guide to Strengthening and Sustaining Organizational Achievement,* Revised Edition. San Francisco: Jossey-Bass Publishers, 1995.

WHAT STRATEGIC PLANNING IS NOT

It is also helpful to understand the limits of strategic planning. Strategic planning is not

- **Written in stone.** Organizations continually have to adjust to unexpected environmental changes. The essence of a strategic plan, then, is not to carve a course of action in stone but to establish organizational practices and approaches to decision making that will be responsive to change. Strategic plans are designed to address long-range goals and to unfold over a three- to five-year period.

- **A departmental, program, or operational plan.** Based on the organizational strategic plan, each department or program will develop its own goals and actions based on vision priorities. These goals or actions provide a more specific roadmap for a group to work from. It is essential that these work plans align with the organizational plan and vision priorities.

- **Something to be updated.** It is tempting to update an existing strategic plan. But updating would really be *incremental planning,* not strategic planning. Incremental planning might take less time, but it has a hidden risk. By planning incrementally, you run the risk of not looking far to the future or assessing what has changed since the plan was written. It would be like taking two steps up the ladder without considering which wall to place the ladder on.

Coats and Ties, a mid-sized nonprofit based in Indianapolis, provides job training and business attire to men who are re-entering the workforce. The organization has a great reputation and hundreds of success stories; it has done a great job serving the needs of the city. But Delilah Simmons, the new chief executive, was wondering if the organization was reaching its full potential and what it should do about helping those in the more rural suburbs, where access to services might be hampered by transportation issues or fuel costs. Does Coats and Ties have the resources to address those needs? *Should* Coats and Ties address those needs? The organization has no real plan for growth, and Simmons is afraid of stagnation. One of the biggest challenges is making the time to have these kinds of conversations within the organization and with her board. She decided it was time to talk to John Daniels, her board chair.

WHY ORGANIZATIONS SHOULD PLAN

Sometimes boards and staff members need to be convinced that strategic planning is worth the investment of money and time. They need to know how the process will benefit them and the organization. Strategic planning can provide enormous benefits. It can

- *Bring clarity and agreement on mission and vision*
  Agreement on mission (the organization's purpose) is paramount. Without this agreement, an organization cannot be effective. The strategic planning process can provide an invaluable opportunity for dialogue and consensus among staff, board, and volunteers. Defining a shared vision (the organization's future direction) and then planning based on that desired outcome is the essence of strategic planning.

- *Help organizations prepare for the future*
  As the popular saying goes, "If you don't know where you're going, you'll probably end up someplace else." A strategic plan outlines the steps to achieve a desired future for an organization. It is comforting for board, staff, and volunteers to have a roadmap to follow. The planning process prioritizes the work to be done. Strategic planning facilitates making short-term decisions based on long-term implications. Most important, a strategic plan provides a series of agreements about what needs to happen. A plan is a dynamic and flexible document that can be adapted to accommodate change.

- *Help organizations anticipate and manage change*
  Planning allows an organization to anticipate change and prepare for it. Planning also helps an organization deal with unexpected changes in its environment.

- *Improve decision-making processes*
  With a strategic plan in place, day-to-day decision making and problem solving will be directly related to long-range and short-term goals. Planning reduces stress by making decisions easier. When choices are made within the context of a strategic framework, the organization's direction is clearly defined. If there is no strategic framework, the future of the organization is in the hands of whoever is making choices. Strategic decision making and problem solving assure that the organization's vision will be achieved.

> "Instead of being confident in our plans, we can be confident in ourselves. What does it mean to be confident in yourself? In part it means believing in your own ability to take a long view and act accordingly. It means knowing that you are prepared for anything — that you have maneuvering room no matter what happens, that you can make meaningful choices and will not have to be a complete prisoner of circumstances."
>
> — Peter Schwartz, *The Art of the Long View*, New York: Doubleday, 1991.

- *Promote effective stewardship*
  Practicing good stewardship means being accountable to others. Clients and funders of a nonprofit charitable organization assume they will pay for services or donate money, respectively, to the organization, which will re-invest the revenues to address the social need. Similarly, association members and foundation board members and grantees assume that funds will be used for the greatest impact. Because strategic planning helps nonprofit organizations fulfill their missions, it also helps them be stewards of the public's trust.

- *Align the board and staff*
  When there is shared purpose and direction ("we're all in the same boat"), there is the basis of a high-performance team. When individuals are focused on the same goal or outcome, they feel a certain amount of synergy and often set aside differences, help each other, and become invested in a common purpose. An organization's mission cannot be achieved without board members and staff who agree on a common direction and are committed to achieving success.

- *Provide an opportunity to recommit to the cause*
  Focus on the future work of the organization can bring the board, staff, and other stakeholders into alignment around the mission. Group interaction around a cause often fuels individual commitment.

- *Educate participants about institutional history*
  By producing a synopsis of significant events in its history, an organization learns what has worked and what has not worked. Historical synopses might include a description of major milestones and changes that have contributed to how the organization functions today. Understanding the past enables choices about what it can become in the future. This document can also be valuable in orientation of new staff, volunteers, and board members.

- *Identify existing strengths*
  Customer feedback conducted in conjunction with the plan indicates how well the organization is meeting expectations. It can also show where efforts are paying off and what to celebrate.

- *Provide an opportunity to analyze the systems and processes*
  It is valuable to conduct a critical review of the organization's processes and how it operates. A review provides an opportunity to make improvements. Pay particular attention to communication channels and cross-functional operations.

John Daniels took great pride in his work with Coats and Ties. He spent a lot of time talking about the organization, encouraging people to volunteer, and occasionally meeting with clients of the organization to offer advice and support. Daniels believed that preservation of this necessary institution was his primary responsibility as board chair, and he took that responsibility seriously. When Simmons approached him about her thoughts on expanding the organization, Daniels had more questions than answers. Was it appropriate for the organization to expand? Will we need more staff? More real estate? If so, how do we attract adequate funding? Will our current funders, volunteers, and staff support this? What's the real need in these areas? If we don't expand, what's the alternative? What does the rest of the board think? Daniels decided to broach the topic at the next board meeting and recommend that the chief executive create a dedicated task force to begin the process of strategic planning.

If you don't know where you are going, then any road will do.

Cheshire Cat, from *Alice in Wonderland*

WAYS TO ADDRESS COMMON CONCERNS AND COMPLAINTS

Getting buy-in to do strategic planning is not always easy. Indeed, the chief executive should be prepared for resistance from some staff and board members. Here are common roadblocks board members and staff raise to oppose strategic planning.

> *Communicate throughout the process.*
> - *Distribute the process map.*
> - *Post a "thermometer" or other graphic that shows progress.*
> - *Include strategic planning updates in a weekly or monthly newsletter.*
> - *Send broadcast emails after each meeting.*

"We didn't have a good experience in the past."

For all those who have experienced the benefits of successful strategic planning, there are others who found the process burdensome. When the process is clearly defined in advance, people tend to find it less confusing and threatening. Show participants that it includes a commitment to regularly monitor progress on goals, which will likely have a significant impact.

"We don't have time to do this right now."
There is a certain irony in this since the frequency of crises declines when there are effective strategies to follow. Help people understand the long-term benefits. Point out ways that the strategic plan will make daily decisions and prioritization easier.

"We don't understand how all the parts fit together."
What is often missing is a sense of the order in which these steps will unfold and how they will come together in the "big picture." In the beginning, give people a roadmap of the planning process. Assure them that they will have the opportunity to respond to the goals and actions being proposed.

"Strategic planning is exhausting."
Comprehensive planning is time consuming, but the discussions that take place during the process are the very conversations that effective, well-managed organizations should conduct on a regular basis if they want to be successful.

"We will just have to do this all over again in a few years."
Sadly, many organizations complete the lengthy process of strategic planning only to watch the final plan disappear into the office archives. A few years down the road, with new board members and new staff members, someone challenges the organization to, once again, revisit the entire process. If the original plan, however, includes mechanisms for continuous monitoring and evaluation, its recommendations will become integrated into the permanent organizational DNA.

When you are satisfied that board and staff members are ready to begin planning, you will want to think of ways to incorporate the process of planning into the daily life of your organization. Throughout the process of planning, remember to communicate, communicate, communicate.

A nonprofit is most effective when all parts of the organization are aligned with the shared mission and goals. Over time, as external conditions change, different parts of the organization may lose this alignment. To combat this tendency, organizations need to re-examine themselves — what they are and how they work. Strategic planning allows the time and dialogue for assessment. Written plans become reminders of agreements made during the strategic planning process, but the promise of shared strategic thinking and behavior is more important than completed, written plans.

An organization creates its own future through effective planning, becoming more proactive than reactive to the workplace and marketplace. As management guru Peter Drucker said, "The best way to predict the future is to create it."

CHAPTER 2
THE PHASES OF STRATEGIC PLANNING

The development of a strategic plan unfolds in a series of discrete phases, with each step building on the one that came before.

1. Planning to plan
2. Understanding the context of the organization (history, trends, client perceptions)
3. Agreeing on the organization's purpose and direction
4. Moving from vision to action
5. Monitoring progress on the plan

PHASE 1 — PLANNING TO PLAN

Phase 1	Phase 2	Phase 3	Phase 4	Phase 5
Planning to Plan	Understanding the Context	Agreeing on Purpose and Direction	Moving from Vision to Action	Monitoring Progress

The chief executive must decide how the organization will go through the planning process and prepare the staff and board. Begin by addressing the following questions:

1. Is our organization ready for strategic planning?
2. What is our history of planning?
3. How will we facilitate the process?
4. Who will we include in the planning process?
5. What kind of human and financial resources do we need?

1. IS OUR ORGANIZATION READY FOR STRATEGIC PLANNING?

Nonprofits experience a variety of phases in their life cycles, including new chief executives, significant shifts in the context of their work, and major changes in funding. In these times of turbulence, a well-crafted plan can afford an organization time to focus on what is truly important. The steps in the planning process don't change. Some steps may take longer given an organization's circumstances, e.g., if it is between leaders.

Strategic planning often requires the board and staff to tolerate a level of vulnerability as they go through the process. Participants should trust each other before beginning the process because negative feedback and criticism are common. An organization should be stable before beginning the strategic planning process; if it is going through a chief executive transition, you should postpone strategic planning until a chief executive is in place. The selection of a chief executive may be based in part on an existing strategic plan. The time is likely to be ripe for change, presenting an exciting opportunity to create a new plan. (See Chapter 3 for more discussion of the roles in the strategic planning process.)

The chief executive should be sensitive to the fear among staff members that their jobs may be in jeopardy as organizational infrastructure is evaluated. A facilitator or consultant directing the planning process can help allay these fears and address them by creating a comfortable and trusting environment.

An organization that is experiencing significant conflict probably does not have the necessary trust between staff and board to have a successful strategic planning process. If this is the case, you should postpone the strategic planning process until the conflict is resolved.

> Simmons had heard from other chief executives that strategic planning could be a blessing and a curse. Some people swore by planning, conducting the process every three to five years or so; others complained that their boards were disengaged or that the plan just sat on a shelf. Coats and Ties was just four years old, and there was no history of this sort of process. With the board's recommendation in hand, Simmons selected five of her employees to participate on the strategic planning task force. She took care to pick people with a variety of skills and experience, searching in particular for employees who had been through the process with another organization. While there were initial concerns about the additional work load that the task force would represent, Simmons was pleasantly surprised by the level of enthusiasm for the project. A few members of the task force noted that staff members are "so full of ideas, we won't be able to write them down fast enough!"

There are also external factors to consider. Is the organization's relationship with external stakeholders steady enough to withstand feedback? Is the sector within which the organization operates in turmoil? If so, it may be wise to postpone planning until the internal and external environments are more stable.

Preparing Board, Staff, and Volunteers for Strategic Planning

The board should be a strong advocate for strategic planning and should be prepared to be involved in the process. Because the board is removed from day-to-day operations, it may have a tendency to be less committed to the status quo; therefore, it may bring a broader perspective. Since the board is responsible for seeing that the mission is fulfilled and for ensuring adequate funding, it should want the organization to perform at the highest level.

Today, participative planning includes board, leadership, and staff (sometimes paid *and* unpaid staff) in helping define strategy. People support what they help create; when they have been a part of the strategic planning process, they feel more ownership of the plan.

Answering the following questions will help board and staff think about planning. These questions may be presented in a survey or discussed at board or staff meetings.

- What are the most important issues that we are dealing with right now?
- What do we think needs to be improved in our organization?
- What concerns us most about our organization?
- How can we better enact our mission?
- How effectively are we marshaling resources, especially time and money?
- How open are board and staff to change?
- What are some barriers to getting people involved in the planning process?

2. WHAT IS OUR HISTORY OF PLANNING?

- What are the lessons learned from past planning efforts?
- Have there been previous strategic plans?
- How have they been utilized?
- What were the outcomes?
- Can the positive results be replicated and the negative ones minimized?

3. HOW WILL WE FACILITATE THE PROCESS?

- Is there someone in our organization with well-developed facilitation skills? Remember, there is a difference between facilitation skills and content expertise. Effective facilitation prohibits involvement in the substance of strategic development but requires focus on the process.
- Should an outside consultant be retained to facilitate the process? Chapter 3 covers hiring a consultant, and Appendix VII offers guidance on choosing a consultant.

4. WHO WILL WE INCLUDE IN THE PLANNING PROCESS?

Participants can include staff, leadership, association members, grantees, volunteers, board members, clients, peers, and community partners. As the number of people involved increases, so does the richness of the input to the plan. People who are "involved" have an opportunity to provide input to the process. But that does not mean they need to attend any or all planning meetings or write the plan.

Unless the organization has a very small staff, it is advantageous to create a strategic planning task force. A task force is different from a committee, which may be formed in perpetuity. Using a task force assumes that the group will dissolve once its work is complete. A task force will champion the organization through the planning process by:

- designing the planning process for the organization (who, what, when, and how)
- ensuring the process is followed to completion
- communicating progress regarding the strategic planning process

Recruit members of the strategic planning task force by getting representatives of various cohorts within your organization. The simplest way to do this is to create a chart with the criteria you want to consider. Brainstorm names, fill in their criteria, and select a diverse group. Both the board chair and the chief executive should serve on the task force. (See Appendix I for a sample chart.)

When convening the Strategic Planning Task Force, make sure everyone is clear about the expectations. (See Appendix II for a template to charter a strategic planning task force.)

5. WHAT KIND OF HUMAN AND FINANCIAL RESOURCES DO WE NEED?

The amount of staff time and financial costs of strategic planning often come as a surprise. Some stakeholders may argue that items such as staff time, meetings, and the services of a facilitator are prohibitively expensive. This is understandable, since people are naturally cautious about investing for the sake of desirable, yet intangible, future outcomes.

How should the chief executive address this issue? One approach is to break the process into the five phases discussed in this chapter. This makes the cost of each phase manageable and the anticipated benefits more immediate. By following this approach, direct costs may be more in balance with benefits. As the process produces tangible and positive results, it will garner support to enter the next stage. It is important to be realistic about the cost of the process, including compensating an outside facilitator and paying for meeting space, amenities, staff time, and committee and board meetings. The following questions will help assess the resources necessary for planning.

- How much staff time can be devoted to planning?
- What is the cost/investment (time, resources) to the organization?
- Is there money in the budget for an outside consultant to guide the process?
- Is there money in the budget to conduct research?
- What will it cost to gather feedback from our stakeholders via surveys, focus groups, and interviews?
- Is there a venue to hold the meetings?
- What equipment and materials will be needed?

KICKING OFF THE PLANNING PROCESS

The official beginning of the strategic planning process can take many forms. It all depends on who your audience is. Most organizations benefit from a more visible announcement of the event.

The kick-off announcement and/or event can:

1. Officially begin the process
2. Educate staff and volunteers about the strategic planning process
3. Model the participatory nature of the strategic planning process
4. Communicate what will happen and how all individuals will be involved
5. Make strategic planning an organizational priority
6. Have a rallying effect, bringing energy to the process

Good communication is a critical component of the planning process. A useful tool to use throughout the process is a Communication Action Register (see Figure 6, page 38).

PHASE 2 — UNDERSTANDING THE CONTEXT

Phase 1	Phase 2	Phase 3	Phase 4	Phase 5
Planning to Plan	Understanding the Context	Agreeing on Purpose and Direction	Moving from Vision to Action	Monitoring Progress

In order to fully understand the context in which your organization exists and to evaluate the various forces that affect its present and future, it is important for the strategic planning task force members to compile, synthesize, and absorb information about the organization's external and internal environments.

Analysis that combines information from external environmental assessments with an appraisal of the organization's internal dynamics (such as the strengths, weaknesses, opportunities, and threats, or SWOT, analysis) identifies the current and future context of the organization. For the layout of a SWOT analysis, see Appendix IX and the accompanying CD-ROM.

ANALYZING EXTERNAL CONTEXT

One of the most important components of the process is, ironically, one that is most often inadequately performed — the survey of external factors that affect the organization. Unless these factors are analyzed, you risk having a plan that is unbalanced with excessive emphasis on internal factors.

In scanning the external environment, the planning task force should ask the following questions:

- What opportunities and threats does the organization face? Key leaders can get together to brainstorm opportunities and threats.

- What do external stakeholders (clients, partners, community) need or expect from the organization? There are a number of methodologies for getting input from external individuals. For a list of data-gathering methods, see Appendix III.

- How well does the organization perform relative to its competitors (competition for clients, volunteers, support, etc.)? Define who your competition is and how well your organization performs by comparison.

- What are the trends in the world, country, region, state, and community that will have impact on the work of your organization, and how should you respond to those trends in the planning process? Create a Trend Analysis to understand trends that will affect the work of your organization. List the trends that are most significant, and then describe what the organization should do to respond. For a Sample Trend Analysis, see Appendix IV.

ANALYZING INTERNAL CONTEXT

Historical data about the organization's past provide valuable information on the internal forces that shape its future. The historical synopsis might include a description of major milestones, events, or changes and the impact those have had on your organization. These might include a change in:

- leadership
- membership
- mission
- economic status
- funding
- programming
- personnel
- location
- equipment
- accountability
- community involvement
- organization's environment/culture/climate

Once you have compiled those key pieces of historical data, pose the following questions:

1. What does our history tell us we do well?
2. What does our history tell us we should abandon?

The organization also needs feedback on how those working with the organization perceive it. Ask paid and unpaid staff for their perceptions of the organization. See Figure 1 on the following page for a list of questions to ask internal stakeholders.

Figure 1
STAFF AND VOLUNTEER SURVEY

History	• What events have shaped our organization? • What do we do well that we should continue to do? • What activities, programs, and practices should we abandon?
Values	• What are our organization's values? • How well are our organization's values defined? • Are behaviors consistent with the stated values? • What are some formal or informal, spoken or unspoken, "rules" in our organization that may be causing problems or holding us back?
Leadership	• How do you feel about the way decisions are made? • When making decisions, do our leaders try to balance quality of life for employees with cost or productivity? • In what ways do leaders walk the talk? • How open are leaders to disagreement with their ideas, plans, etc.? • Do our leaders support you? If so, how well?
Empowerment	• Do you have the resources to do your job effectively? • Does the organization encourage risk taking? If not, what are the consequences of taking risks? If so, what are the rewards? • Are you able to freely and creatively meet your constituents' needs without repercussions?
Communication	• Are communication channels open between you and co-workers? Between leadership and staff? • Do the organization's leaders communicate critical information (results, successes, failures, problems, future plans) on a regular basis? • How is conflict dealt with? • Are diverse opinions encouraged?

INTERNAL STAFF AND VOLUNTEER SURVEY (CONTINUED)	
Vision/Strategy	• How clear are you about the vision and direction of our organization? • How connected do you feel your work is to the overall strategy of our organization? • How do you gauge customer satisfaction? • How would you rate the emphasis on customer satisfaction? • How do you feel about quality and quantity of work in our organization?

A strategic plan is only as good as the understanding of the context in which the organization operates. Taking the time to fully understand context reduces uncertainties in the strategic planning process and will give the plan greater credibility with constituents. Investing time to understand context saves time and money in the long run. This phase of strategic planning may uncover new ideas and provide new opportunities to connect with stakeholders or even new communities.

Understanding the organization in context is the foundation for defining problems or opportunities and for designing a plan to address them.

PHASE 3 — AGREEING ON PURPOSE AND DIRECTION

Phase 1	Phase 2	Phase 3	Phase 4	Phase 5
Planning to Plan	Understanding the Context	Agreeing on Purpose and Direction	Moving from Vision to Action	Monitoring Progress

Once the chief executive and the task force understand the context in which the organization operates, it is time to address questions regarding the vision and mission. The task force should address foundational agreements such as:

- Why does the organization exist?
- What will be the ultimate result of its work?
- What are the values that the organization's members share?

The mission and vision statements summarize an organization's purpose and direction. Along with its values, they encompass its fundamental purpose and philosophy. While the statements may be brief, the information in the mission and vision statements is crucial. It constitutes the DNA of the organization — the master templates from which specific actions and programs evolve. Both statements describe why the organization was created and its ultimate dream for the future. No wonder mission and vision statements are hard to write!

When creating and reviewing a mission statement, think about why the organization exists, not what it does or how it works. For example, rather than claiming, "ACT provides food, clothing, and money to support villages in Southwest Uganda" (how), the mission statement might read, "ACT is an organization of people dedicated to improving the spiritual, physical, economic, and societal conditions of communities." That is the reason the organization exists.

A vision statement describes an ideal future for the organization, not the social cause that it addresses. So, a council for child abuse and neglect should describe what its organization will look like in five years: "We are a strong, integrated system providing innovative programs and comprehensive services affecting generations to come" rather than "end child abuse." The vision statement of a statewide school board association reads: "We are the recognized and respected voice of public education, leading through demonstrated expertise, active and engaged membership, and superior service in a competitive, global environment." The statement, written in the present tense, creates a vision of what is yet to be accomplished. Although the school board association is not yet fully recognized, it "sees" itself as the voice of public education, and its vision statement reflects that.

Organizational values are lasting and enduring; they stand the test of time. When times get difficult, an organization doesn't shed its values. It embraces them to help weather the storm. Values are not just beliefs. They are also behaviors that can be observed. When people say they value collaboration, their behavior should reflect that value.

Values should be unique to each organization. In some cases, the values of the organization may be the only standards that set it apart from the competition. It is incredibly powerful for the board and staff to agree on the behaviors they will expect of each other and for which they will hold each other accountable. Agreeing on values defines the "gold standard" of how the board, staff, and volunteers will work together and treat constituents. It makes sense to write down or review the organization's values during the strategic planning conversations because values, like strategy, express bigger, longer-term views of the organization.

PHASE 4 — MOVING FROM VISION TO ACTION

Phase 1	Phase 2	Phase 3	Phase 4	Phase 5
Planning to Plan	Understanding the Context	Agreeing on Purpose and Direction	Moving from Vision to Action	Monitoring Progress

SET VISION PRIORITIES

After agreement on the mission and vision, the next phase is to agree on five to seven important areas of focus in order to achieve the vision. These areas of focus are called vision priorities, and they give concrete form to the abstraction of the vision statement. Here are some examples of vision priorities.

- The coalition has adequate funding to sustain its efforts.
- We changed our culture to be more prevention-focused.
- We defined and established a formalized statewide coalition.
- We created a statewide identity.
- We defined specific outcomes with data to prove our value as an organization.
- We obtained sufficient resources.
- We use the most up-to-date technology for recruitment, fundraising, advocacy, and meetings.
- We created a "volunteer presence" in every community in the state.
- We are a motivated, dedicated, diverse team that recognizes the intrinsic value of each individual.
- We establish and maintain strong, collaborative relationships with all our partners.
- We use innovative strategies to secure adequate resources to support our organization's projects.

Most organizations have five to seven vision priorities.[2] It is difficult to focus on more. The important question to ask when finishing the list of vision priorities is, "If we achieved all these vision priorities, would we have achieved our vision?"

ASSESS THE INFRASTRUCTURE

With the mission, vision, and vision priorities defined and agreed to, the next step is for the strategic planning task force to view the organization as a living system. Every organization is composed of different individuals and groups working on

---

[2] Based on work done with 225 nonprofit clients in 21 years by Cornerstone Consulting Associates, LLC.

specific programs and services. Changes in any one part of the system usually affect other groups. Strategic planning often uncovers changes that "have no home" in the current infrastructure. For example, a statewide public health administration identified marketing as a vision priority but, after viewing its infrastructure against the vision priorities, realized there was no specific group dedicated to this function. In another organization, a board of directors may realize a long-standing committee no longer has relevance given the current strategy.

The purpose of this review is to ensure that the way you are organized to do the work today will support the vision priorities you have identified for tomorrow. Questions to address include

- What are the functions in the organization (financial, programmatic, support, etc.), and how do they relate to each other?
- How well will our current infrastructure enable us to achieve our vision priorities?
- Are there any functions missing?
- Do we have functions we no longer need?

DEFINE GOALS AND ACTIONS

Based on the vision priorities, the participants should create goals that must be completed to achieve each priority. For example

Vision priority: We are nationally recognized among professionals and policymakers.

Goal: Design and implement a comprehensive marketing plan by year's end.

Vision priority: We achieved more sustainable and diversified funding.

Goal: Establish sustained giving through cause marketing and other strategies in two years.

Each vision priority might have between three and 10 goals. Once goals have been agreed upon, they should be prioritized, and the organization should determine how many of them are achievable in the first year of the strategic plan. Next, the goals should be written. The first-year goals and actions make up an annual plan. Because much can change in a year's time, you should wait to write the actions for goals beyond the first year. Annual plans for subsequent years should include goals not yet achieved and actions for achieving those goals.

"Actions" in a strategic plan will make up the day-to-day responsibilities of staff. The actions become the most specific statements in the plan and include who will champion the action, who will be involved in its execution, what resources are needed to complete the action, what the timeframe is, and how will the action be measured. Actions based on the above examples include

Vision priority: We are nationally recognized among professionals and policymakers.

Goal: Design and implement a comprehensive marketing plan by year's end.

Action: Determine the budget, timeframe, and criteria for hiring a consultant to complete a marketing plan.
Champion: [Name]
Who could be involved in this action? [Name]
Resources: [Money, space, equipment]
Action Deadline: [Date]

Vision priority: We achieved more sustainable and diversified funding.

Goal: Establish sustained giving through cause marketing and other strategies in two years.

Action: Research other programs of sustained giving, and select the model most suitable to our organization.
Champion: [Name]
Who could be involved in this action? [Name]
Resources: [Money, space, equipment]
Action Deadline: [Date]

For mor examples of organizational vision priorities, goals, and actions, see Appendix V.

Completing the Strategic Plan

All strategic plans share the same intent — to provide effective direction and operational guidance to board and staff members of the organization as they conduct their daily business.

It is helpful to provide portions of the plan to individuals both inside and outside the organization. Versions of the plan may vary depending upon who receives it. The staff and volunteers who are responsible for implementing the goals should receive the entire document. Because the board will be responsible for monitoring the plan's implementation, board members will be more focused on the vision priorities and the goals than on the actions to achieve the goals. If possible, provide the board with an executive summary that focuses on the high-level priorities and goals, as well as a full copy of the plan.

Likewise, funders and community partners may not need all the details of the goals and actions but may find that having the shared mission, vision, values, and vision priorities is pertinent to their role. Other members of the community could receive an executive summary, depending on the organization's relationship with them. For more information on the finished written plan, see Chapter 4.

PHASE 5 — MONITORING PROGRESS

Phase 1	Phase 2	Phase 3	Phase 4	Phase 5
Planning to Plan	Understanding the Context	Agreeing on Purpose and Direction	Moving from Vision to Action	Monitoring Progress

Strategic planning does not end when the plan has been written and distributed. On the contrary, strategic planning never ends.

A well-formed strategic plan will guide decision making and help ensure that all activities and programs are aligned with the organization's mission. The plan also is meant to be a functional tool that can evolve with changing circumstances.

Therefore, ongoing monitoring and revision are two important aspects of effective strategic planning. This continuous process includes

- incorporating the vision priorities, goals, and actions of the strategic plan into program and individual work plans and budgets
- reviewing overall performance of the organization against its plan on a periodic basis and making appropriate revisions

In Phase 5 of the process, the strategic planning task force will develop appropriate evaluative metrics for regularly reviewing performance and include them in the plan. The plan itself should be evaluated quarterly. Procedures for periodic review allow for corrective action at regular junctures in order to maintain the momentum of the plan and to maximize effectiveness of operations in accomplishing goals and actions. Strategic planning is never over. It is a cyclical process in which continuous evaluation demands reality checks and regular adjustment. (See Figure 2 on the following page for a suggested monitoring approach that the chief executive can use.)

Ongoing attention to the plan should also occur in a less formal way at regular organizational events such as staff meetings, committee meetings, and individual performance reviews. The chief executive should encourage staff members to refer to the strategic plan to ensure that all actions are still in line and that no aspects of the plan have been neglected. The board naturally should do the same when reviewing staff reports.

Figure 2
MONITORING THE STRATEGIC PLANNING PROCESS

What	How	Who	When
Regularly review goals and actions	Report progress at staff meetings; conduct project reviews once a month; review progress of goals and actions as part of staff performance evaluations		
Keep mission and vision front and center	Begin all meetings with review of mission and vision; talk about how mission came alive this past week/month; identify how daily work supports vision		
Measure performance against values	Annually evaluate board and staff on behaviors that adhere to values		
Report on progress toward vision priorities	Conduct quarterly comprehensive reviews of vision priorities at board and leadership levels; review progress of vision priorities as part of chief executive performance reviews		
Report on changes to strategic plan	Adjust goals and actions to reflect actual work; renegotiate actions and timelines; revise, update, and publish plan annually		

PLANNING TIMEFRAME

Typically, time demands on the participants can lead to a desire to compress or eliminate certain steps in the process. Skipping steps always results in a cost to the final plan. If pressure to cut corners arises within your organization, be very cautious about eliminating any of the steps. They are there for a reason!

Depending on the size of your organization, this five-phase planning process may take more than two and a half days to three months or longer. The longer allows ample time for each step in the process and some additional time in between. It also spreads out the steps into more manageable pieces — for example, a shorter meeting to gather the input during Phase 2: a meeting to agree on the purpose and direction and vision priorities; and writing and prioritizing goals. At each meeting, ensure that the environment is conducive to creative thinking, with flipcharts to record ideas and plenty of wall space to hang the large pieces of paper. Figure 3 — Suggested Timing of Meetings through the Five Phases, provides a glimpse of the steps, stakeholders, and time required.

Figure 3
SUGGESTED TIMING OF MEETINGS THROUGH THE FIVE PHASES

Meeting 1	Chief executive, board or selected board members, selected staff/volunteer leadership	• Identifying the desired outcomes for strategic planning for the organization. • Determine who needs to make up the strategic planning task force. • Completing the charter for the task force.
Suggested time between meetings: 3 weeks to recruit and determine task force membership.		
Meeting 2	The strategic planning task force	• Understand and agree on charter. • Get to know each other and the roles on the task force. • Plan the kick-off.
Suggested time between meetings: minimum of a few days.		

Meeting 3	The strategic planning task force	• Determine how to complete the external and internal context.

Suggested time between meetings: 4 weeks or more to complete surveys, analyze results and complete the reports on the context.

Meeting 4	The strategic planning task force	• Review the context reports and determine how to distribute this information to everyone coming to the next meeting. • Plan the next meeting logistics.

Suggested time between meetings: 3 weeks or more to invite participants and prepare for the next meeting.

Meeting 5 (might be two meetings)	The entire board, the strategic planning task force and any other stakeholders the task force invites	• Agree on shared mission. • Agree on shared vision. • Agree on vision priorities. • Agree on values.

Suggested time between meetings: 1 week or more

Meeting 6	The strategic planning task force (or assigned teams/programs)	• Examine infrastructure for alignment with the strategy. • Write goals based on each vision priority.

Suggested time between meetings: 1 week or more.

Meeting 7	The strategic planning task force (or assigned teams/programs)	• Prioritize the goals for what will become the next year's roadmap in the five-year plan. • Write actions based on the goals selected for the first year.

Suggested time between meetings: 2 weeks or more.

Meeting 8	The strategic planning task force	• Determine how to publish the plan – who gets what version. • Determine how to distribute the plan and celebrate.
Suggested time between meetings: 2 weeks		
Meeting 9	The strategic planning task force	• Create a process that the organization will follow to ensure the plan is driving the work of the organization and gets reviewed. • Celebrate the work of the task force.

If an organization wants to complete a strategic plan in a weekend, some steps will have to be greatly abbreviated, if not eliminated. Figure 4 shows an abbreviated process.

Figure 4
ABBREVIATED STRATEGIC PLANNING PROCESS

Purpose of Meeting	Length of Meeting
Phases 1 and 2: Understanding the context (facilitated in the meeting or prior to the meeting)	2 hours
Phase 3: Agreement on purpose, direction, vision priorities, and goals	4 – 6 hours
Phases 4 and 5: Prioritize goals and write the actions; adopt the plan and create a monitoring process	6 hours

Obviously, the organization must decide how important the planning process is and allot the appropriate time. When you allow a generous amount of time, planning will be more comprehensive, more stakeholders can be involved, and better data can be collected and analyzed. The shorter the process, the less time there is for dialogue and buy-in.

Desire for Instant Results

It is natural for people to want to see results right away, but it is important to establish realistic expectations. The ability of the plan to produce significant results is directly proportional to the time spent on the process of formulating the plan. An organization that invests in a one-day retreat cannot realistically expect to produce as comprehensive a plan as one that devotes extensive time to the process. There is nothing wrong with devoting a single day to a planning retreat if that fits your organization's agenda, but it is important to be clear in advance about the outcomes. Small-scale planning and retreats devoted to assessment of specific aspects of the organization's future have their place. Full-scale strategic planning is a major endeavor that need not be part of every annual action calendar. However, it is important to realize what can be accomplished during meetings and short retreats. Unrealistic expectations result in disappointment.

THINGS TO REMEMBER ABOUT THE PLANNING PROCESS

In the hierarchy of plans, the strategic plan is the backbone that supports the rest of the organization's plans. Other plans, such as individual or personal plans, and department, financial, fundraising, marketing, and program plans, should be derived from and in alignment with the strategic plan.

Your plan should be flexible enough to be adapted to the changes in your organization and the environment. The strategic plan is a living document. In order to remain relevant to the work of the organization, it must change from time to time — not on a whim, but in a measured approach that examines how each change will affect the other parts of the plan.

The annual plan is based on the strategic plan and is composed of the current year's prioritized goals and actions. Drafting the annual plan from the strategic plan provides a convenient opportunity to bring out the master plan and verify its relevance. The overall strategic plan must be able to outlive annual plans. Otherwise, the planning process has failed to see past the next calendar year and capture any possible trends shaping the future. A solid plan is well anchored in the future yet flexible enough to absorb regular review and occasional changes — before the next major review changes the priorities.

Once a year, the board and staff leadership should come together to

- focus on the accomplishments of the year
- reflect on the relevance of the mission and vision
- discuss the relevance of the vision priorities in today's environment
- prioritize goals for another year

This annual planning meeting can be the opportunity to celebrate accomplishments and reinforce the organization's commitment to achieving its mission.

A nice adage to keep in mind for planning is: "Go slow to go fast." In other words, take the time to determine the right process for planning for your organization, and then devote the appropriate amount of time and emphasis to it.

CHAPTER 3
PARTICIPANTS' ROLES AND RELATIONSHIPS

Strategic planning is a team effort. Without appropriate input and feedback from all stakeholders — individuals who either depend on or benefit from the services provided by the organization or who ensure support by financing, overseeing, or implementing the activities — it is difficult to address all of the organization's options. But just as a coach doesn't put the entire team on the field at once, different stakeholders may contribute at different times in the planning process.

The first part of this chapter describes the people on the team — including an outside facilitator — and the roles they might play. Even with great people on your team, it will be a challenge to make the experience a good one for everyone, while managing the process and ensuring that the outcome is a top-notch, functional plan. The second half of this chapter addresses what's involved in achieving balance among the people, the process, and the output or plan.

KEY STAKEHOLDERS AND THEIR ROLES

THE CHIEF EXECUTIVE

The chief executive's responsibility is to ensure agreement on the organization's goals and methods of achieving those goals. Within this context, the chief executive drives the planning process. She typically takes the lead in recognizing the need for strategic planning and determining whether the time is right to initiate the planning process.

The chief executive's responsibilities are

- *Enlist support for strategic planning from board members.*
  Agreeing on the organization's mission and vision is one of a board's basic responsibilities. The chief executive ensures that the board is involved with setting the direction for the organization. The board chair's support is particularly important since her active engagement in the strategic planning task force is a key factor in the success or failure of the process. If the board chair or board members resist participation, the chief executive must seriously consider how the board views its roles and responsibilities to the organization and should ask the board chair to initiate a review of those roles and responsibilities or to have a private conversation with a reluctant board member.

- *Define participants and their roles.*
  The chief executive determines who should be included in the planning process. With help, she also defines the role of each participant, determines the point in the process when each participant will be involved, and ensures that there is clear communication among the different players so that everyone is informed of progress. Having internal and external participants is beneficial. Internal participants have an obvious stake in the organization's future and have day-to-day knowledge of what works and what doesn't. External participants can bring a fresh and possibly unbiased perspective and different areas of expertise.

- *Prepare board and staff for planning.*
  As the driver of the process, the chief executive will tell board members and staff members what is expected of them and how and when they will contribute. It may be necessary to educate and coach them throughout, not just in the beginning, and remind staff members that they will have to step away from day-to-day activities in order to participate in the "big-picture" aspects of planning. This orchestration by the chief executive will help alleviate confusion and misunderstandings.

- *Coordinate and integrate participants' input, and provide regular updates.*
  The chief executive is the main communicator, and her role is to ensure that consistent, current information is available to everyone on a schedule that will reinforce the logical sequence of the planning steps. She should also acknowledge each milestone, as it is achieved. It is not necessary for the chief executive to *write* each communication, but each one should come from her. See Figure 6 on page 38 for an example of a Communications Action Register.

- *Manage and contribute to the process.*
  The chief executive makes it clear when action is needed and ensures accountability and a timely completion of the process. She is also an active contributor and listens to all sides of an argument. This is a difficult position that requires patience and perspective in order to be neither too passive nor too dictatorial.

Together, the chief executive and board will

- *Determine whether to include an outside consultant in the process.*
  To help ensure that all participants may contribute to the process without leadership bias, it may be advantageous to engage an external facilitator. (See Appendix VII, How To Choose a Strategic Planning Consultant.) The consultant reports to the chief executive.

- *Decide who will be on the strategic planning task force and what the responsibilities will be.*
  The task force typically includes the board chair, key board members, staff executives, and staff members who will be responsible for implementing various aspects of the plan. Always include at least one person who ultimately has authority to make decisions that affect implementation of the strategy.

The responsibilities of the strategic planning task force include

- Ensure that appropriate stakeholders are involved.
- Conduct research and obtain relevant information.
- Ensure that the planning process does not get sidetracked and is completed.
- Produce and review the final written plan.

THE BOARD

Board participation is vital to developing the strategic plan. As the link between the organization and its environment, the board can help reconcile the ambitions of leaders and staff with the constraints of economic and political realities. This important role makes it imperative that board members offer their different perspectives but eventually find consensus on strategy.

Beyond the development of the plan, there are benefits to having the board involved in the process. The strategic plan will eventually guide the board in decision making, facilitate and inspire the board's fundraising efforts, and help the board better understand how the organization operates. The vision priorities from the strategic plan can become the basis of board agendas, dialogue, debate, and decision making.

The board's responsibilities in strategic planning are

- Set the direction of the organization.
- Balance short-term needs with long-term goals.
- Assume responsibility for the completion of the planning process and outcomes.
- Work with the chief executive to provide guidance and input in developing the strategic plan.
- Represent the organization's diverse constituencies within the strategic planning task force, with special emphasis on the community that the nonprofit serves.
- Add value to discussions by sharing their expertise in legal, financial, marketing, technological, industry-related, and business areas.
- Provide information about topics such as governance practices, program offerings, organizational initiatives, and technical developments based on their experiences on other boards.
- Offer counsel on the impact strategic initiatives will have on the organization's fiscal viability and fundraising capacity, and make sure the right questions are asked.
- Approve or adopt the plan.
- Periodically monitor the implementation of the strategic plan.

THE STAFF (PAID AND UNPAID)

The staff is responsible for the details of operational planning, constituting the link between the top-level vision of the organization and its everyday activities. Having key staff and volunteers on the strategic planning task force is important for several reasons. Staff members work on programs and interact with clients and constituents. Mixing board members and senior staff during planning sessions allows them to share their unique perspectives, better understand their respective concerns, and build trust. Furthermore, through staff involvement in the planning process, the people who ultimately will implement the activities of the plan have a chance to shape it and buy into its initiatives.

The responsibilities of the staff in the strategic planning process are

- Provide background information, research, data, and institutional history.
- Bring their unique perspective of programs and services.
- Provide professional and subject-matter expertise.
- Ensure the plan is realistic, given their day-to-day work.
- Keep the mission and vision alive throughout the organization, ensuring that the organization has a sense of shared mission and vision.
- Offer administrative support to the strategic planning task force.

CLIENTS/CUSTOMERS

Just as customer research drives strategy in the for-profit sector, clients, customers, members, and funders of a nonprofit organization can provide valuable input to its strategy. Constituents' perceptions of an organization are often different from those of the board, chief executive, or staff. Gathering information on these perceptions provides an opportunity to monitor quality and client/customer satisfaction. Appendix III suggests methods for obtaining this information.

John Daniels sat in a board meeting looking over some of the feedback from staff and volunteers about the role of Coats and Ties in the greater community. He was both pleased and shocked at the level of passion in the responses. Clearly, staff and volunteers had strong feelings about the future of the organization, and they had suggested ways to improve the organization's activities.

The organization had hired a firm to conduct brief interviews of some past and present clients, and some of the comments were upsetting. It seemed the organization wasn't adequately tailoring its training to job opportunities in the area. The client remarks were harsh and direct. One past client, echoing a popular sentiment, felt that the training program at Coats and Ties "set me up for a job that was outsourced eight months later."

> Delilah Simmons explained to the board that the organization had never tracked data for repeat customers, and that they measured job acquisition but not job retention. These client interviews clearly highlighted the need for a new approach to measuring success at Coats and Ties. Armed with these revelations, Delilah felt sure that the strategic planning process would now be much stronger because they had hard data on which to base some of their decisions.

COMMUNITY PARTNERS

Many nonprofits are creating strategic partnerships with other nonprofits and, in some cases, public/private partnerships to share costs, services, or personnel. For example, two county health departments share an administrative staff and building to save costs. These partners can become important stakeholders in the planning process and can provide meaningful input. Use the methods provided in Appendix III to ask for input from your community partners.

CONSULTANT/FACILITATOR

Although it is possible to develop an effective strategic plan using a staff member to manage the details, it is sometimes advisable to employ an outside strategic planning consultant/facilitator. This decision makes particular sense if the organization is doing strategic planning for the first time.

The primary reason for using an outside facilitator is to provide neutrality. A staff member will naturally have a vested interest in the outcome of some of the issues being discussed and may even unknowingly create a meeting agenda that will affect the outcomes.

There are two types of consultants to consider: strategic planning consultants and neutral facilitators.

- Strategic planning consultants have expertise in the steps, nuances, and desired outcomes of the strategic planning process and have meeting facilitation skills; they can also gather and analyze data. Consultants can offer orientation and training to the members of the strategic planning task force to maximize their efficiency, and they can use their experience to help streamline the process and avoid common pitfalls.

- A neutral facilitator can run the planning meetings and maintain a neutral position about the content, allowing staff to focus on content rather than process.

With either of these choices, the dedicated task of the strategic planning consultant/facilitator is to keep the process on track.

The main functions of a consultant/facilitator involve moving the process forward and ensuring that adequate information is available for educated decision making. The consultant/facilitator usually doesn't offer input or opinions about outcomes or the quality of decisionmaking.

The strategic planning consultant/facilitator should

- work as a partner with the organization, serving as the expert in process design
- facilitate meetings and create a safe environment to have strategic conversations
- identify what information is needed for planning
- understand the context within which the organization functions
- conduct interviews and research in the internal and external environment
- synthesize and analyze information for easier consumption
- guide task force discussions
- understand to whom she reports

For additional information on how to choose a consultant, see Appendix VII.

The strategic planning task force should determine when and how to involve each person or group. Board involvement usually will be required in establishing the organization's mission, vision, and values. Staff involvement will be required in analyzing the organization's current issues and operational goals. The staff and volunteers determine specific actions required to meet strategic goals. Mixing the board and senior staff during planning helps board members understand day-to-day issues of the organization and helps the staff understand longer-term issues. It also helps build relationships among all those who are invested in the future of the organization.

Appendix VI is a worksheet for listing stakeholders and when and how to involve them in the strategic planning process.

ACHIEVING BALANCE IN THE PROCESS

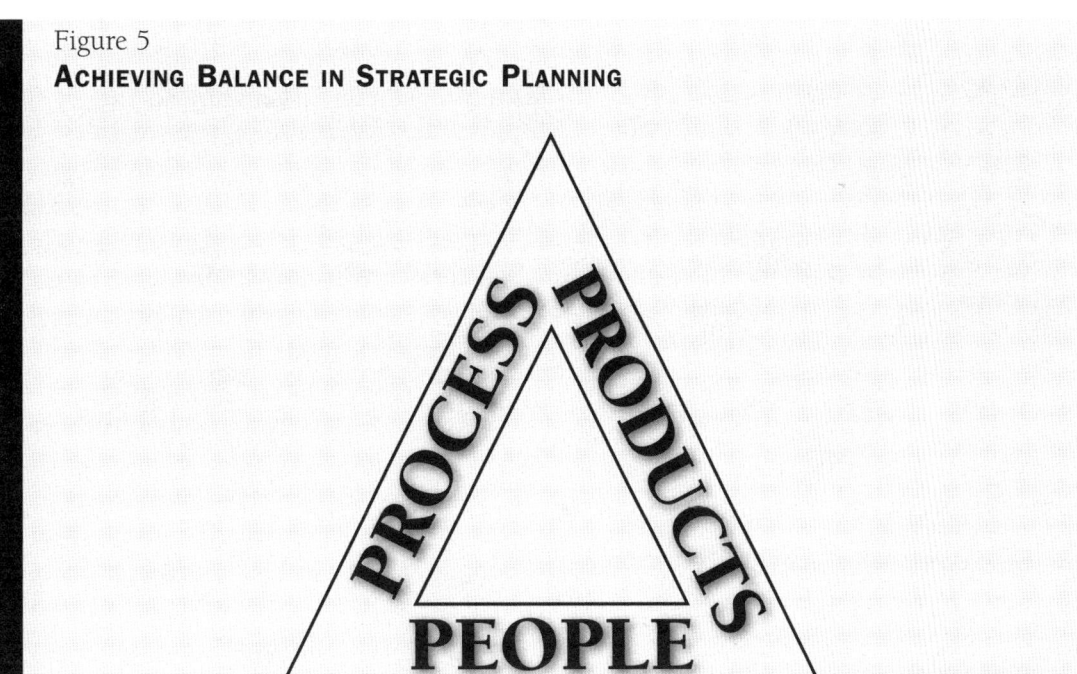

Figure 5
ACHIEVING BALANCE IN STRATEGIC PLANNING

Maintaining balanced group interactions in meetings is vital to sustaining the momentum of the planning process and to achieving success. It is helpful to think of a triangle when illustrating the fundamental principle of balanced group interactions (Figure 5). Each side of the triangle represents a key component of the planning group's interaction — process, people, products (results) — that must stay in balance with the other two. If one of the components is overemphasized or underemphasized at the expense of the other two, the triangle is no longer balanced, and group effectiveness suffers.

Over short intervals, however, the balance among these three components can be disrupted legitimately in order to address an area of focus. For example, if there are difficulties with the group dynamics, the facilitator might choose to focus on the people component at the expense of the other two components. Eventually, however, balance must be regained.

In effective group interactions, products (results) are not more important than people (relationships), which in turn are not more important than process (efficiency). All three, equally balanced, create the foundation for healthy group interactions. One way to check for balance is to make sure all three components are equally represented when you put together meeting agendas.

COMMON OBSTACLES IN PLANNING

- *Missed Deadlines*
  Continually missed deadlines are evidence that the priority for planning is low. Is there a legitimate explanation, or is there an organizational crisis? Does the timeline need to be revised? Was it realistic? A planning process that is drawn out over too long a period loses momentum and commitment. You may need to get renewed commitment from key players.

- *Poor Communication*
  To avoid a breakdown in communication and ensure that relevant parties are kept informed, it is advisable to implement a communications process that systematically manages the information flow. See Figure 6 for an example of a simple method for documenting stakeholder involvement. This table can be used at the end of each meeting of the strategic planning task force to ensure that decisions and other relevant information are disseminated to the right stakeholders at the right time.

Figure 6
COMMUNICATION ACTION REGISTER

What stakeholders do we need to communicate with?	What are the outcomes they need to hear about from this meeting?	Method of communication (verbal, written, formal, informal)	Who will communicate from this team?	By when?

- *Inability to Reach Consensus*
  Consensus is essential to strategic planning. Consensus is defined as an agreement that everyone is willing to live with and will actively support after the meeting.

  Few things are more frustrating than thinking you reached a consensus only to discover soon after that the agreement has fallen apart. What happened? Although it may not have been evident, there was probably silent opposition to the agreement from staff or board members who did not object at the time but subsequently undermined the agreement by speaking negatively about it to others.

False agreements are destructive to the dynamics of the planning process and can even threaten the very foundations of the plan. It is essential to confirm agreements at every critical juncture. To help ensure that you have agreement:

1. Clearly restate a proposed agreement in front of the whole group.

2. Check for understanding. Is everyone in the room interpreting the agreement in the same way? Does everyone agree on the same definition of words used? If there is disagreement, define important words or substitute new words. Do this "reality check" at each key point in the overall process. This is an especially helpful technique when crafting the words used in the shared mission and vision.

3. Ask for agreement from each individual. Verify person by person around the table that each agrees with the statement as written. If someone says no, ask: "What would it take to gain agreement?" Often, only a minor adjustment is required.

In some situations, consensus is beyond reach. At that point, the strategic planning facilitator should ask if the group will consider a majority vote, and try to reach consensus around the vote. A vote can resolve an issue and allow the task force to move on and keep up momentum and progress. The down side is that there may be perceived winners and losers, which can be detrimental to goodwill within the group. Some of the losers may become disgruntled and not participate fully in the process.

- *Unequal Participation*
  Participative planning assumes that all or most individuals in the organization contribute in one way or another. To address this issue, be certain that the right stakeholders are at each meeting and the facilitator is encouraging input from everyone there. Be sure to show how people's contributions have positively affected the process.

- *Conflict*
  When you bring a diverse group of people together to plan, there may be conflict. Conflict in and of itself is not bad; in fact, it can foster critical, strategic thinking. The challenge is in managing conflict so it doesn't derail the meeting. These tactics will help

    - Keep the conflict about the content or issue, not the people involved. When it sounds personal, bring it back to the issue or concept.

    - Ensure that participants are focusing on the longview and what's best for the organization as a whole. Too often people become territorial based on their stake in the organization.

CHAPTER 4
COMPONENTS OF A STRATEGIC PLAN

The strategic plan is the record of agreements that have been reached through the strategic planning process. The document is by no means the sole purpose of the process; it is simply the first concrete indication that your planning has reached a measurable junction. The written plan contains the guidelines for future action for your organization based on data that the organization has and assumptions it makes.

It works best to have just a few people involved in compiling and writing the plan. You may want to consider delegating this task to staff members who have played key roles on the task force. As internal stakeholders, they have a vested interest in writing a clear document. After all, the staff will have to interpret the plan on a daily basis. If you have hired a consultant/facilitator to lead your planning group, you may engage the consultant to assist in compiling the plan.

The format of the plan largely depends on the culture of your organization. There is no standard formula. Some organizations have a one-page document; others have a complex manuscript with charts and tables to illustrate key points. Factors to consider are the complexity of your organization, environmental factors that need to be mentioned, the sophistication of the industry standards that regulate your activities, and financial constraints. The rule of thumb for each organization is: Keep it straightforward and clear. A plan that continually needs interpretation is not doing its job properly. Figure 7 offers an outline of the main elements in a comprehensive strategic plan. Figure 8 contains a simple version.

WHO GETS WHAT VERSION OF THE STRATEGIC PLAN?

Consider tailoring different versions of the strategic plan to meet individuals' and stakeholder groups' needs. The strategic planning task force can determine this. For instance, board and staff will need a complete version of the plan to implement it and monitor progress. Community partners may need a condensed version including the mission, vision, vision priorities, and values.

Figure 9 lists possible components of the plan and matches them to different stakeholders or stakeholder groups. Go down each column for each stakeholder group and check the boxes by the content you think that stakeholder group needs. This will show you how many versions you need to produce and disseminate.

Figure 7
COMPONENTS OF A STRATEGIC PLAN (COMPREHENSIVE VERSION)

Introduction

    A letter from the board chair and/or chief executive supporting and introducing the plan

The Context for Planning

- Historical synopsis of the organization
- Internal and external customer feedback results
- Trend analysis of external environmental factors

Purpose, Direction, and Principles

- Mission and vision statements
- Value Statement
- Vision priorities for reaching the vision
- Goals that support each vision priority

The Current-Year Plan

- The goals prioritized and the goals for the first year of the plan delineated
- Actions that support the prioritized goals
- Documentation of the formal adoption of the strategic plan

Monitoring Progress

- The process that will be used to monitor progress on the plan

Figure 8
COMPONENTS OF A STRATEGIC PLAN (SIMPLE VERSION)

1. Mission and vision statements
2. Vision priorities for reaching the vision
3. Prioritized goals and actions for the first year
4. Process that will be used to monitor the plan

Figure 9
MATCHING THE COMPONENTS TO STAKEHOLDERS

Components	Stakeholders/Stakeholder Groups			
Table of contents				
Letter from board chair and/or chief executive supporting the plan				
Charter to the strategic planning task force				
Historical synopsis				
Customer feedback				
Trend analysis				
Mission				
Vision				
Values				
Vision priorities				
Goals that support the vision priorities				
Prioritized goals				
Actions that support prioritized goals				
Documentation of final adoption of plan				
Process for monitoring the plan				
Testimonials from the strategic planning task force about the process				

Coats and Ties ended up with a plan to address some gaps in the job training program, create partnerships with other organizations to reach the surrounding suburbs in the short term (with the possibility of establishing a more permanent presence there in the future), and implement a client feedback and analysis system. The plan wasn't exactly what Delilah Simmons imagined it would be, but both she and the board felt that at the conclusion of the planning process, Coats and Ties would be a stronger organization. Taking the time to plan was exhausting, but the result seemed to energize staff and volunteers alike.

CONCLUSION

The intention of this book is to increase the nonprofit chief executive's understanding of and appreciation for the strategic planning process. Keeping the following points in mind will help you have a successful process.

- **Give your organization a head start.** A nonprofit with a strategic plan in place has a head start on the future. Planning will not eliminate every issue in an organization, but it gives an advantage in solving problems. There may be *excuses* for why an organization fails to plan strategically, but there is no good *reason*.

- **Bring energy and a proactive mindset.** Organizations that have significant conversations about their future and produce an effective strategic plan have a greater sense of collective energy and focus. They are always thinking about ways to move closer to their shared vision. The organization becomes proactive rather than reactive to the constantly changing workplace and community need.

- **Demonstrate leadership.** In periods of significant social and economic change, when many of the past assumptions on which organizations were built appear to be breaking down and resources are limited, it is even more important for nonprofit chief executives to provide decisive leadership. It is indeed challenging to develop a strategic plan when major uncontrolled forces, such as steep economic decline, hover on the horizon and threaten your future, but the presence of those forces makes planning even more essential.

- **Maintain focus.** Putting your organization on a continuous cycle of planning and evaluation ensures that it will stay focused on fulfilling the mission and achieving the vision. An investment in strategic planning serves to align the different parts of the organization by providing a common, unifying perspective. In times of tight budgets, staff should be concerned not just with saving money but with taking actions that maximize the impact of limited resources on strategic objectives.

- **Control your destiny.** An organization with a plan is likely to end up where it wants to be. One without a plan risks splintering into disparate pieces. The ultimate benefit of engaging your organization in a strategic planning process is that it gives all stakeholders a real chance to shape the future — instead of being overwhelmed by it.

- **Strengthen your board.** In addition to ensuring that your organization is not only climbing the ladder efficiently but has it placed against the right wall, the strategic planning process will lead to numerous other positive changes in the organization. The board will have the opportunity to add value by engaging in an activity that enhances the organization's future impact. Participating in such an important endeavor is bound to increase board members' satisfaction about their service and naturally feed into stronger board commitment. With a strategic plan in place, the board agenda can be built around vision priorities, ensuring that all board discussion is strategic in nature.

- **Invest in your team and reap the dividends.** An involved staff is a confident staff. Close collaboration with staff during strategic planning gives individual staff members a sense of being appreciated and considered vital participants in the future of the organization — not just implementers of board wishes. With input comes buy-in. Participation generates accountability — the more someone knows, the more she is accountable for what she knows.

Finally, strategic planning permits clients, members, and other participating stakeholders to get to know your organization better, thus increasing their loyalty. Listening to their feedback allows you to better focus on their needs. By fulfilling the needs of your constituents, your organization has the best chance of fulfilling its mission and achieving its vision. And that is the purpose of strategic planning!

APPENDIX I
RECRUITING THE STRATEGIC PLANNING TASK FORCE

When recruiting members for the strategic planning task force, try to get the most representative group possible. Determine the criteria that are important to you and then brainstorm some obvious names for the left-hand column. Monitor diversity by putting information into the columns to the right.

The ideal group size varies from organization to organization, but many successful groups have 7 to 15 members. Having more than 15 makes scheduling difficult.

Names of potential members	Age group	Gender	Length of time with organization	Functional area of expertise	Position in organization

APPENDIX II
CHARTERING THE STRATEGIC PLANNING TASK FORCE

Just as a boat needs a charted course, the task force needs a charter that provides clear direction to the team members on all aspects of their journey together. A team is more likely to succeed if members have clarity and agreement about

- why the group exists
- what they are expected to accomplish
- who they are responsible to
- what the team can and cannot do
- what the key tasks or responsibilities are

A team charter is a written agreement that defines the team, establishes its purpose, clarifies authority, and gives the team direction for its collective work.

SAMPLE CHARTER DOCUMENT

TASK FORCE IDENTITY (HOW THIS TEAM WILL BE KNOWN IN THE ORGANIZATION)

Strategic Planning Task Force

TASK FORCE MISSION (PURPOSE)

Example: The Strategic Planning Task Force exists to champion our organization through the planning process by

- designing the strategic planning steps
- ensuring that the process is followed to completion
- communicating progress regarding the process
- evaluating and improving the planning process for future use

TASK FORCE VISION (DESIRED OUTCOMES)

Example: The vision of The Strategic Planning Task Force is to involve all levels of our organization in a continuous cycle of planning; facilitate the process of defining our common direction, of defining the steps to get there, and of creating the steps to implement and monitor the plan.

TASK FORCE MEMBERSHIP

The members of the Task Force are:

The Task Force Sponsor is: [sponsor is the person or group that is ultimately responsible for the task force, e.g., the board of directors or chief executive]

Sponsor's Role: [usually represented on the task force]

TASK FORCE AUTHORITY

What this task force can do: (sample wording below)

Example:

1. Recommend future directions

2. Discuss issues surfaced during the planning process and delegate to the appropriate person or department

What this task force cannot do:

Example:

1. Commit financial and staff resources

2. Communicate directly with the media without going through the proper channels

TASK FORCE MEMBER ROLES AND RESPONSIBILITIES

What tasks will be accomplished and by whom: (i.e., recorder, distribution of meeting notes, meeting logistics)

TASK FORCE INTERFACE WITH OTHERS

How this task force will communicate with other individuals and teams:

(See Figure 6, Communication Action Register.)

TASK FORCE GROUND RULES

Example:

- Keep a long-term focus on what is best for the organization.
- Talk about the planning process outside our meetings and maintain a positive message about it.
- Keep things pertinent to this team confidential.
- Make meeting attendance a priority, and follow up on assigned actions.

TASK FORCE DECISIONMAKING

Consensus is a decision that everyone is willing to live with and actively support. If consensus cannot be reached, then the team will vote based on a simple majority to move the team forward.

TASK FORCE TIMEFRAME

The authority of the task force will end when the planning process is complete and implementation of the plan has begun.

Date of charter: _____

APPENDIX III
METHODS OF GATHERING INPUT

Method	Overall Purpose
Questionnaires, surveys	To quickly and/or easily get lots of information from customers in a nonthreatening way
Interviews	• To fully understand someone's impressions or experiences • To learn more about their answers to questionnaires
Documentation review (application, finances, memos, minutes, etc.)	To get an impression of how a product/service operates without interrupting the process or service
Data analysis and/or observation	To gather accurate information about how a product/service is delivered, particularly about processes
Focus groups	To explore a topic in depth through group discussion

Advantages	Challenges
• Can complete anonymously • Can easily compare and analyze data • Can administer to many people • Can use sample questionnaires that already exist	• Asking the right questions • Wording can affect customer's responses • Surveys are impersonal • May not get the full story
• Can get full range and depth of information • Can develop relationship with customer • Can be flexible for customer	• Asking the right questions • Takes a lot of time • Can be hard to analyze and compare data • Can be costly • Interviewer can introduce bias into customer's responses
• Can get comprehensive and historical information • Can obtain information without interrupting service • Can use information already existing • Can get information with few biases in the process	• Often takes much time • Information may be incomplete • Being clear about what information is needed
• Can view actual operations as they occur • Can adapt to events as they occur	• May be difficult to interpret "seen" behaviors • Can be complex in categorizing observations • Can influence behaviors of program participants
• Can quickly and reliably get common impressions • Can be an efficient way to get range and depth of information • Can convey key information about programs	• Asking the right questions • Can be hard to analyze responses • Needs a good facilitator for safety and closure • Can be difficult to schedule groups of people • Can be costly to hire a professional to run

APPENDIX IV
SAMPLE TREND ANALYSIS

Instructions:

Agree on a list of trends that will have significant impact on the work of your organization, for example:

- geographic shifts
- state, local, or national policies or mandates
- technology changes
- demographic shifts
- staffing patterns
- budgetary/funding changes
- financial projections
- business changes
- customer shifts
- competitive environment
- collaborative relationships
- trends specific to your industry or field of expertise

Once you have identified the trends you want to include, add them to the first column in the table on the following page, then cite the source of the trend information and capture possible responses that your organization should have to that trend.

Trend	Source of the Trend	Implications for our Organization
1. Increased emphasis for collaboration	NACCHO article; Collaboration for a New Century	• We need to proactively explore partnerships for grants and funding. • We need to look for potential cost savings (e.g., benefits, administrative costs).
2. Increased emphasis on outcome measurement and accountability	Centers for Disease Control and Prevention, 2009	• We need to define program outcomes and measure the impact through data collection. • We need to train staff to do this.
3.		
4.		
5.		
6.		
7.		

APPENDIX V
SAMPLE VISION PRIORITIES, GOALS, AND ACTIONS

Vision priorities and the vision statement are typically written in the present tense, as if they have already been achieved.

Sample 1

Vision priority: As a healthy, viable organization, we are building and utilizing strategic partnerships.

Goal: We network and collaborate with others who share similar goals at the local, state, and national levels to leverage opportunities.

Action: Create a list of potential partners and prioritize which ones to contact. (Action Champion, others involved in this action, resources needed to complete the action, timeline)

Sample 2

Vision priority: We have adequate staffing, paid and unpaid, for display, education, and events.

Goal: Create a staffing plan for the next five years ensuring coverage for all areas in our strategic direction.

Action: Have staff managers review their staffing needs and submit them to the chief executive.

(Action Champion, others involved in this action, resources needed to complete the action, timeline)

Sample 3

Vision priority: We have sustainable and broad-based funding.

Goal: Maximize funding and reimbursement or revenue streams, increase operational and administrative efficiencies, and stay within budgeted expenses.

Action: Implement new fee collection structure for optional medical and dental procedures

(Action Champion, others involved in this action, resources needed to complete the action, timeline)

Sample 4

Vision priority: We have dedicated efforts to build expertise and research-based information.

Goal: Complete a trend analysis; gather existing best practices to put a system in place.

Action: Contact other associations to learn how they record their expertise and how they compile research-based information.

(Action Champion, others involved in this action, resources needed to complete the action, timeline)

APPENDIX VI
WORKSHEET FOR INVOLVING PARTICIPANTS

The planning team can use this worksheet to:

1. consider all the potential individuals or groups that could participate in the strategic planning process
2. decide how they could participate and at what point in the process
3. generate ideas for getting and keeping them engaged

Participant	Activities and When to Participate	Comments

APPENDIX VII
HOW TO CHOOSE A STRATEGIC PLANNING CONSULTANT

Consultants are a varied lot with different strengths and approaches. It is important to find the right one for your organization. The Association of Management Consulting Firms considers the essential assets of a qualified consultant to be

- extensive experience and ability
- specialized knowledge and technical skills in special functional or technical areas
- impartial viewpoint for a fresh, unbiased approach to difficult problems
- confidential handling of sensitive situations

Retaining a consultant to conduct strategic planning should be viewed as the formation of a partnership. Successful consultant-client partnerships do not just happen by accident. Rather, they result from a preliminary set of mutually agreed upon expectations, which define how both parties intend to proceed. In order for the partnership to work, the chief executive and the consultant must agree that they and the stakeholders participating in the planning process will be honest, frank, and candid. See Appendix VIII for a sample agreement between a consultant and a nonprofit chief executive.

GENERATING A LIST OF CANDIDATES

Start by asking trusted peers and colleagues for recommendations. Broaden the list by requesting recommendations from similar organizations in your region, from staff at your organization's national office, from relevant professional associations, and from your funders. When conducting research, be sure to ask how familiar the source is with the accomplishments of the consultant. Request references from the candidates for the same type of work completed with other clients, and take the time to call and get feedback on their work.

Some organizations issue a Request for Proposals, or RFP, to narrow the list of consultants. This is more common for government-funded projects or large-scale engagements. If you do not consider RFPs necessary, be sure to cast a wide net in search of qualified consultants, and spend time grading applications according to specified prerequisites. It is most effective to reduce the list to three consultants for interviews.

INTERVIEWING

There are many similarities between the initial interview and a hiring interview, so conduct it the way you would typically interview an employment candidate. Both the chief executive and board chair should interview the candidates, as should other significant stakeholders as desired.

EVALUATING

In rating the candidates, organize evaluations into the following categories:

Personal Characteristics

- Does the consultant's style fit comfortably with that of your organization? Are the consultant's personal strengths aligned with your organizational culture?
- Is the consultant clear and concise in written communication?
- In verbal communication, is the consultant clear and lucid or ambiguous?
- How well does the consultant listen?
- Does the consultant answer questions with direct or vague answers?
- Does the consultant show interest in the organization's situation or more interest in promoting himself or herself?
- Does the consultant seem authentic? Do you have a sense that "what you see is what you get"?
- Does the consultant respond quickly to your requests?

Preparation and Results

- Has the consultant taken the time prior to the interview to learn about your organization?
- Can the consultant articulate his or her planning philosophy? Does this philosophy fit with yours?
- Can the consultant articulate your organizational needs and describe your situation?
- Does the consultant inquire about your timing or budget constraints?
- Does the consultant provide examples of completed plans? Evidence of successful implementation?

Process

- Is the consultant willing to adapt his or her planning process to your organization, or will you be forced to fit into the consultant's process?
- Does the consultant bring references from similar planning projects?
- Are staff members given the same attention and respect in interviews as the chief executive and board members?

REFERENCE CHECKS

Asking for references is much more than a formality. Valuable information will be obtained that can reinforce or challenge the judgments made during the interview.

Here are some questions to ask when checking references:

- How did the planning project work out? Were the desired results accomplished?
- Would you hire this person again?
- Would you recommend this person to a trusted colleague?

MAKING THE COMMITMENT

After selecting the consultant, put agreements into writing. (See Appendix VIII for a sample agreement.) Ideally the consultant will write the scope of work to be included in the agreement, including

- Accountability: Who is responsible for what?
- Deliverables: Define the agreed-upon outcomes — not just process
- Time frames and due dates
- Process management:
    1. How communication will be managed
    2. How confidentiality will be managed
    3. Key organizational contact for the consultant (avoid multiple contacts) and how the consultant will get support from other staff members

The consultant you choose to guide your strategic planning process will determine how smoothly the process functions and how well equipped you will be to implement the new directives for your organization. Spend the time necessary to find the right match.

APPENDIX VIII
SAMPLE CLIENT–CONSULTANT AGREEMENT

On behalf of [client]:

- The [leader] of [client] fully supports initiating strategic planning as evidenced by participation in meetings and agreements.

- The [leader] of [client] understands that the control of sharing information will shift somewhat to the facilitator of the process. Typically, people more freely and honestly share when there is a third party facilitating. This is part of the objectivity that we can provide your organization.

- The board chair fully supports initiating strategic planning as evidenced by participation in meetings and agreements.

- The board devotes at least 30 minutes of an agenda to a presentation by the consultant on strategic planning.

- The planning team members understand that because it is their organization, they will have to do the most important work.

- The leaders in [client] demonstrate the priority assigned to the process by freeing people to participate (staff time, board time, financial resources).

- The [client] exhibits tolerance for change.

- The leaders in the [client] demonstrate the priority assigned to the process by setting dates for the whole process into the calendar (at least tentatively).

On behalf of [consultant]:

- The consultant will document the expectations of the client and regularly refer to them.

- The consultant will advise the organization when the process is being altered in a way that prevents these outcomes and the process outcomes from being achieved.

- The planning team, after discussion with the consultant, understands that:

- Because this is such an open process, areas of discontent, if they exist, may be shared by members of [client] and "customers."
- The members of [client] will become somewhat vulnerable in their sharing during the process.
- The members in [client] will expect trust to increase in [client] as a result of their willingness to be open and participate.
- Some new communication processes sometimes get defined (i.e., newly chartered teams) to support the [client's] future strategies.

- The consultant will pursue an agenda through our expertise and knowledge of the content and process of strategic planning. We will pursue that openly, while respecting the strategies of [client].
- The consultant will offer important opinions in our work with [client].
- The consultant will be fully present in the maximum, appropriate way. We will not be present when we believe that the client can accomplish the outcomes without our involvement.

On behalf of both [client] and [consultant]:

- The consultant and the planning team will consider themselves partners throughout the process.
- The consultant and the planning team will define and tailor the planning process that supports both [client] and the outcomes.
- The consultant and the planning team will talk frequently and openly during the process. We will both strive for the best two-way communication.
- We will promote confidentiality, when needed, for greater participation in the process by members of [client].
- We don't always know what we will encounter together in this process, but we will be honest with each other.

APPENDIX IX
ABOUT THE CD-ROM

The CD-ROM contains the PowerPoint® presentation *Presenting: Strategic Planning.* This set of predesigned slides (and other accompanying material) is designed to help chief executives explain and present different types of strategic planning their boards.

The slides are in Microsoft® PowerPoint® graphics presentation format and can be used as an on-screen presentation or printed as overhead transparency slides or handouts for the board. The CD-ROM also contains additional files with presentation notes and talking points. Use some or all of the sections depending on how they apply to your nonprofit and the time you have allotted for the presentation.

The CD-ROM includes a file describing each of the sections in the presentation as well as a file with step-by-step instructions for customizing the PowerPoint® slides.

SUGGESTED RESOURCES

Allison, Michael, and Jude Kaye. *Strategic Planning for Nonprofit Organizations, Second Edition.* New York: John Wiley & Sons, 2003.

Axelrod, Nancy. *Chief Executive Succession Planning: Essential Guidance for Boards and CEOs, Second Edition.* Washington, DC: BoardSource, 2010.

Berry, Brian. *Strategic Planning Workbook for Nonprofit Organizations, Revised and Updated.* St. Paul, MN: Amherst H. Wilder Foundation, 1997.

Brinckerhoff, Peter C. *Mission-Based Management: Leading Your Not-For-Profit in the 21st Century.* New York: John Wiley & Sons, 2000.

Bryson, John M., and Farnum K. Alston. *Creating and Implementing Your Strategic Plan: A Workbook for Public and Private Nonprofit Organizations, Second Edition.* San Francisco: Jossey-Bass Publishers, 2004.

Drucker, Peter F. *The Five Most Important Questions You Will Ever Ask about Your Nonprofit Organization: Participant's Workbook.* San Francisco: Jossey-Bass Publishers, 2008.

Eadie, Douglas. *Changing by Design: A Practical Approach to Leading Innovation in Nonprofit Organizations.* San Francisco: Jossey-Bass Publishers, 1997.

Grace, Kay Sprinkel, Amy McClellan, and John A. Yankey. *The Nonprofit Board's Role in Mission, Planning, and Evaluation, Second Edition.* Washington, DC: BoardSource, 2009.

Kotler, Philip, and Alan Andreasen. *Strategic Marketing for Nonprofit Organizations.* Englewood Cliffs, NJ: Prentice Hall, 2007.

Strategic Planning: Design for the Future. Special Edition of *Board Member*®. BoardSource, May 2002.

Tucker, Glenn H., Kermit M. Eide, and Jean S. Frankel. *Building a Knowledge-Based Culture: Using 21st-Century Work and Decision-Making Systems in Associations.* Washington DC: ASAE, 1997.

Waechter, Susan A. *Organizational Planning.* Midland, MI: Cornerstone Consulting Associates, LLC, 1993.

ABOUT THE AUTHOR

Susan Waechter works to present the best options for future development to her clients in areas such as integrating system-wide strategic planning and improving board effectiveness and leadership. Waechter has 35 years of leadership experience in the nonprofit sector. She has worked with more than 250 nonprofit clients — primarily leading them through strategic planning and leadership development in government, healthcare, education, social service, and the arts. She is past vice-president of the International Board of Directors of the Association for Volunteer Administration (AVA); a board member on several nonprofit boards; a member of BoardSource; the American Society of Association Executives (ASAE); the Michigan Nonprofit Association (MNA); and qualified to administer the Myers-Briggs Type Indicator. She has co-authored two additional books: *Change: Meet It & Greet It,* and *Flip Art: A Practical Guide to Graphically Improve Your Flipchart Presentations.* Waechter holds a bachelor of arts degree in liberal arts from the University of Kansas.